Isaiah 53

Who is the
Suffering Servant?

The Challenge of the Ages

By Frederick Alfred Aston

ISBN: 978-1-78364-489-6

www.obt.org.uk

****

THE OPEN BIBLE TRUST
Fordland Mount, Upper Basildon,
Reading, RG8 8LU, UK.

Isaiah 53

Who is the Suffering Servant?

Contents

About the author

Frederick Aston was born in Sopockin, Lithuania in 1899 but moved to the USA. He obtained both a bachelor's degree and a master's degree in theology from Princeton Theological Seminary and was ordained by the Presbytery of New Brunswick in 1931. From 1931-1945 he served as the minister of the New York Jewish Evangelism society. In 1946 he was awarded a Doctor of Divinity by the University of Dubuque and served as an evangelist to the Jewish community till his death in New York 1972.

Acknowledgement

The research this treatise necessitated is far out of proportion to its size. A debt of deep gratitude is due to Professor Robert H. Pfeiffer of Harvard University and to Professor Godfrey R. Driver of Oxford University for their invaluable suggestions. My greatest indebtedness is to the Lord.

F.A.A.

Preface

Preface

In the following pages Dr. Aston has rendered a great service to Christian believers. With scholarship and reverence he has challenged the validity of some current interpretations of the fifty-third chapter of Isaiah and has given us an able defence of the earliest Christian understanding of this chapter. To the question, "who is the Suffering Servant?", the Apostolic Church answered, "Jesus Christ".

Jesus Himself seems to have been convinced that He was the Servant. He declared that the words, "And was numbered among rebels" (Isaiah 53:12), must be accomplished in Him (Luke 22:37). After reading Isaiah 61:1-2 in the synagogue at Nazareth, He said, "This day is this Scripture fulfilled in your ears" (Luke 4:21). His answer to the disciples of John the Baptist (Luke 7:22) is also significant in this connection.

The Apostolic Church expressed itself in no uncertain terms. Philip explained to the Ethiopian eunuch of Queen Candace the meaning of Isaiah 53:7-8 (Acts 8:32-35). In Hebrews 9:28 we read, "So Christ was once offered to bear the sins of many" (see Isaiah 53:4-6). Even more explicitly, 1 Peter 2:22-25 echoes Isaiah 53 and applies it to Jesus Christ.

It is good for our souls to return to the sources of our Christian faith and to renew our faith in our Saviour, who "is verily pierced for our revolt", "crushed for our iniquities", and "is wounded for our salvation".

Robert H Pfeiffer

Hancock Professor of Hebrew
And other Oriental Languages
Harvard University
Cambridge, Massachusetts

Introduction

Introduction

We would commend the careful consideration of this publication to everyone who is truly desirous to arrive at the truth in regard to the most serious and important of all subjects, which is here dealt with. By being instructed in science, we could add nothing to the scholarship we find here, by commending it; but scientific training gives competence in following logical reasoning, and to this we give our endorsement. For this pamphlet places in a clear light the greatest moral problem in the universe, namely, how is it that God, when He is just and righteous, can rectify the sinner; and an answer is found by seeking the solution as revealed in the Scriptures.

There are many who make it their boast that they are rationalists, and will not accept anything *contrary to reason*. They turn from religion, *because they think that it requires them to accept much on faith, which is not reasonable*. But when we turn to the great central question which is here discussed, can we suppose that the Judge of all the Earth would do anything irrational? Where then is a solution to be found which does not subvert the attributes of God? For He cannot set aside His justice, so that in His mercy He may pass over our wrong-doing. How we are to be forgiven, we can only hope to know, therefore, by carefully considering what the Lord God has Himself revealed to us, for He only can find the wondrous way. All philosophies of men to account for sin and evil, and their devices in dealing with it, lead to impossibilities, or, in the end, subvert morality itself. *It is the human way which is irrational.* But as the heavens are higher than the earth, so are God's ways higher than our ways, and His thoughts than our thoughts.

Let us therefore, look into the Scriptures, to see the way in which the Lord has guided the Hebrew people of old, by the object-lessons of the sacrifices, and by the teaching of the prophets, to prepare their minds to understand His ways of atonement for sin, thus showing the need for an actual fulfilment as the highest work of the Messiah. It is this which is set forth and explained from the Scriptures in the discussion before us. As it is a matter which vitally concerns us all, may it be read with an honest and true heart, and the desire to perceive the truth.

W. Bell Dawson, M.A., D.Sc.,F.R.S.C.
Laureate of the Academy of Sciences, Paris

McGill University
Montreal, Canada

The Challenge
of the
Ages

The Challenge of the Ages

Hebrew religious poetry is supreme in world literature for its beauty, depth, and moral elevation. In words of epic majesty the fifty-third chapter of Isaiah, considered by many the greatest passage in the Old Testament, presents a portrait of the Suffering Servant of the Lord. Nowhere does the Old Testament contain a more poignant story. It fills us with awe. This Servant holds the key to the greatest moral problem facing man; and his accomplished work in its solution is the challenge of the ages.

I

52:13   *"Behold, my servant prospers and is*
     exalted;
   He is lifted; he is raised high".

14   *Though once we shrank in scorn from*
    him,-
   His visage marred beyond men's,

His body mangled beyond sons' of
men-

15   *Yet now great nations hold him in*
awe;
In his presence kings fall silent,
See what they had never been told,
Perceive what they had never heard.

II

53:1 *Who would believe what we have heard?[1]*
To whom has the arm of the Lord
been revealed?[2]

---

[1] The Hebrew words *lishmu'athenu* literally means "what we have heard", or "our proclamation". But in the context, in view of the words following, *"To whom has the arm of the Lord been revealed?",* and the well known principle of parallelism in Hebrew poetry, the meaning intended here is, no doubt, *"the divine message we have heard"*.

[2] *The arm of the Lord"* here means the Lord's power to save, to accomplish the work of redemption (Cf. lii 10). In Revelation an act of God is experienced. The meaning of verse 1 is :

2   *He grew straight up like a sapling,*
    Like a shoot from desert ground.
No stature, no majesty that we should hail
    him,
        No beauty that we should praise him.

3   *Despised and aloof from men,*
        A man of sorrows, bowed down with
        grief!³
We turned our faces away from his;
        We despised and we ignored him.

III

4   *Surely he bears our load of transgressions*
        And the burden of our guilt.

Who would believe, that is, who would make
inspired response to the divine revelation in
world history coming to us through the saving
power of God?

³ The Hebrew word *holi*, which means "sickness"
has an extended meaning and may also designate
suffering in general, including "grief", and be
symbolic of sin.

And we supposed him to be stricken,
Smitten of God and humbled.

5   *He is verily pierced for our rebellion,*
Crushed for our iniquities.
He suffers for our redemption,
And is wounded for our salvation

6   *All we like sheep did go astray,*
Each following his own path.
The Lord lets fall upon him
The guilt of us all.

IV

7   *Torments willingly and humbly he endured,*
And opened not his mouth.
He was led as a lamb to the slaughter,
Silent as a sheep before its shearers.[4]

8   *By violence and death was he borne away;*
And who is grieved for his fate,

---

[4] See the *Peshito.*[Sometimes called the Syriac Vulgate. It is the standard version of the Bible for churches in the Syriac tradition.]

Isaiah 53: Who is the Suffering Servant?   22

That he was rapt from the land of the
living,
Slain for his⁵ people's rebellion?
9 His grave was assigned among the wicked,
His tomb among evildoers⁶
Though he worked no evil,
And spoke no guile.

V

10 The Lord delights in his sacrifice;
He revives the life laid down for sin's
atonement
A long posterity he shall have;
And he shall consummate the will of
the Lord.

11 From travail of soul to boundless glory,⁷
From suffering to fullness of grace!

---

⁵ So *The Dead Sea Scrolls,* Ms. I of Isaiah from
Cave I of Qumran.
⁶ So *The Dead Sea Scrolls,* Ms. I of Isaiah from
Cave I of Qumran.
⁷ So *The Dead Sea Scrolls,* Ms. I and II of Isaiah
from Cave I of Qumran and LXX.

"My Servant justifies many,
And bears their sin.

12 *In truth I grant him great men for booty,*
And mighty lords for spoil;
Because he let his life blood flow unto
death,
And was numbered among rebels.
Because he bore the sin of many,
And interceded for the guilty.[8]

~~~~~~~~~

A challenging question at once presents itself: "Who is the Servant?" Scholars have advanced two main theories:

1. That he represents the people of Israel.
2. That he is an unknown individual.

---

[8] The translation of the poem follows the rhythm of the Hebrew and is literal, wherever no sacrifice of meaning, or of English idiom and rhythm, is involved.

The Source
of the
Challenge

The Source of the Challenge

1. The Corporate Theory

What picture does the quoted poem give of the Servant? This can be best obtained by analysis, which will reveal the prophecy's basic elements and constitutive principles.

1)   He is portrayed in detailed features as a human personality.
2)   He is an innocent sufferer (vss. 4; 5; 8d; 9c; d; 12d).
3)   He is a voluntary sufferer (vs. 7a).
4)   He is an obedient, humble, and silent sufferer (vs.7).
5)   His suffering springs from love for sinners, including his executioners, who act in ignorance (vss. 4c; d; 7; 12f)
6)   His suffering is ordained by God in love, and fulfils the divine intentional will and purpose (vs. 10).

7)   His suffering is vicarious, that is, substitutionary (vss. 4a; b; 5a; b; 6c; 8d; 10b; 11d; 12e).

8)   His suffering is redemptive and spiritual in nature (vss. 5c; d; 11d).

9)   His suffering ends in death (vss. 8c; 12c).

10) His death gives way to resurrection (vss. 10b; c; 11).

11) His atoning work leads the straying people to confession and repentance (vss. 4-6).

12) His redemptive work, in which suffering, humiliation, and death are central, inaugurates a life of victory and sublime exaltation (52:13; 52:15a; 52:15b; 53:10; 53:11a; 53:11b; 53:12a; 53:12b).

~~~~~~~~~

Can these characteristics be said to designate Israel – viewed historically, or spiritually, or ideally?

(1) Could Israel have been personified in poetic language lacking any hint of allegory? Scripture knows no parallel case where personification is maintained throughout a whole section without intimation of its meaning, but it presents distinct hints in any allegorical passage. Even so liberal a scholar as Bernard Duhm says:

> The Servant of Yahveh is here treated even more individualistically than in any other (Servant) songs, and the interpretation of his person as referring to the actual, or the "true", Israel is here altogether absurd.[9]

(2) Has Israel as a nation been an innocent sufferer? The words in verse 8, *"Slain for his people's rebellion"*, make the application to Israel as the Servant untenable, since "his people's" clearly indicates Israel, and, if the Servant be the actual nation, how can he be stricken for Israel? In Isaiah 1:4, the prophet speaks of Israel as *"a sinful nation, a people laden with iniquity, a seed of evildoers"*, while in

---

[9] Das Buch Jesaja, vierte Auflage, Gottingen, 1922, p.393.

Chapter 42 he states that Israel's affliction is God's judgement for the nation's sins. The synagogue liturgy for the High Holidays embodies the following confession: *"Because of our sins we have been exiled from the land."*

(3) Has Israel been a voluntary sufferer? Never did the Jews voluntarily go into captivity; each exile was the result of a humiliating national defeat.

(4) Has Israel been an obedient, humble, and silent sufferer? George Adam Smith has well observed:

> Now Silence under Suffering is a strange thing in the Old Testament – a thing absolutely new. No other Old Testament personage could stay dumb under pain, but immediately broke into one of two voices – voice of guilt, or voice of doubt. In the Old Testament the sufferer is always either confessing his guilt to God, or, when he feels no guilt, challenging God in argument.[10]

---

[10] The Book of Isaiah, revised edition, London,

No sooner was Israel released from Egyptian bondage, than the nation rebelled against privation in the wilderness,[11] raising its voice in protest. *"My just right passes over unheeded by my God"* (Isaiah 40:27). Even such personalities as Job, David, Elijah and Jeremiah succumbed to the temptation of complaining bitterly against their lot. The subjugation of Jerusalem by Titus in A.D.70 was one of the most stubbornly contested sieges in all human history. At various times the Jewish people revolted against their Persian, Syrian, Roman and Moslem oppressors.

(5) Has Israel suffered in love? Since Israel's suffering was neither innocent, nor voluntary, nor silent, it, consequently, was not "suffering in love".

(6) Has the suffering of Israel been divinely ordained in love? Israel's suffering is the consequence of her transgression, and not of a

---

1927, vol ii, p.375.

[11] Exodus 17:3; Numbers 11:1; Deuteronomy 1:27.

divine plan and divine love (Deuteronomy 28:62-68; Isaiah 40:2b).

(7) Has Israel suffered for other nations? This question is not answered in the affirmative in the Old Testament, or in early rabbinic literature. Yet the idea of substitutionary suffering and atonement has a prominent place in the chapter, being expressed no less than twenty-one times in eight out of twelve verses:

4. *Surely he bears our load of transgression,*
   And the burden of our guilt.

5. *He is verily pierced for our rebellion,*
   Crushed for our iniquities.
   He suffers for our redemption
   And is wounded for our salvation.

6. *The Lord lets fall upon him*
   The guilt of us all.

7. *Torments willingly and humbly he endured,*
   . . . .
   He was led as a lamb to the slaughter.

8. *By violence and death was he borne away;*

. . . .

That he was rapt from the land of the living,

Slain for his people's rebellion?

10. *The Lord delights in his sacrifice;*
He revives the life laid down for sin's atonement.

. . . .

And he shall consummate the will of the Lord.

11. *My servant justifies many,*
And bears their sin.

12. *Because he let his life blood flow unto death,*
And was numbered among rebels.
Because he bore the sin of many
And interceded for the guilty.

(8) Have the sufferings of Israel brought redemption to the world? The sin of man is too great, the holiness of God too sublime, for man

to be able to redeem himself, let alone others. Scripture teaches nowhere that Israel will be redeemed by its own suffering, far less that it will redeem other nations, and especially not that it will redeem them from the power of sin. Nor does it indicate that a few righteous individuals will redeem either Israel or other nations.[12] Israel's sufferings not only failed to *justify* her oppressors, but, as history well attests, led to their *punishment*. Nazi Germany is a case in point. Since Israel's sufferings have never been *voluntary*, they could have no intrinsic moral value and no redemptive power.

(9) Have the sufferings of Israel ended in death? Whether the historic or the ideal Israel be considered, the answer is assuredly negative. Some see the exile portrayed by the figure of death, but this is untenable, since on the contrary, the exile served as a purifying force, strengthening the monotheistic belief of the Jews and their zeal for God. The Jewish people present a striking exception to the usual course of national development and decline. Every nation

---

[12] Cf. Ezekiel 14:14ff.

that played its role contemporaneously with Israel on the stage of the Old Testament history has long since passed into oblivion. But the survival of the Jews is unique, defying fundamental laws observed in the history of the nations. In spite of exile, dispersion, attempts at forcible assimilation, persecution – in spite of liberation and toleration, often more disintegrating than persecution – Israel still maintains her racial identity.

(10) Has Israel experienced a resurrection? Since neither the ideal nor the historic Israel died, there could be no resurrection of the nation.

(11) Has Israel's suffering produced a moral transformation in the nations and caused them to break down in a confession of guilt? This history of the world answers this in the negative. Throughout the ages nations which oppressed Israel were never known to show the attitude expressed in the chapter, where a prominent place is given to confession and repentance.

(12) Has the humiliation of Israel resulted in glorification? Even if death could be taken as a figure for the exile, the restoration thereafter did not lift Israel from extreme humiliation to sublime exaltation. Neither did Israel win many followers among the nations. It must be noted that the missionary zeal of the Jewish people died out in the early years of the Christian era, when they no longer took an interest in winning Gentile converts. The ancient Khazars, prominent among secondary powers of the Byzantine state-system, present an exception. When the Jews were expelled from Constantinople, they carried on missionary activity among them and succeeded in converting the Khazars to Judaism (ca 740).

For Israel to fit into the prophetic picture of a state of pre-eminence, *"He is lifted; he is raised high ... In his presence kings fall silent"*, three things must be true.

    a. Israel must have made a conscious voluntary atonement – an atonement accepted by men as well as God – bringing redemption to the world.

b. As a result of this atonement, *"Because he let his life blood flow unto death"*, Israel must have attained a position of great power and glory in the world.

c. Israel must have made intercession for the transgressors.

Not one of the three is true of Israel, either the real, spiritual or the ideal.

The first theory, that of considering the Servant as a personification of the Jewish nation, meets with further serious objections. It forces the following interpretations: verses 1-10 refer to the Gentile nations; the death of the Servant symbolises the exile, the end of the Jewish national existence; and, finally, the resurrection is a figurative prophecy of the restoration of Israel, to be followed by the conversion of the heathen. The insurmountable objection to these interpretations lies in the need for assuming that in verses 1-10 the Gentile nations are speaking. No Jewish prophet would have represented the heathen as expressing such sublime unparalleled thoughts and exhibiting the attitude described in the passage. Says Hugo Gressmann:

> A penitential psalm in the mouth of the heathen is altogether improbable; the literature of the Old Testament lacks analogous examples.[13]

The view that the Servant means the spiritual element of the Jewish nation also encounters additional obstacles. It may be said that the spiritual Israelites suffered most in the exile and also that they endeavoured to bring the nation to repentance and to spread the knowledge of God among the Gentiles. They probably met with persecution at the hands of other Jews during the exile. But it is hard to believe that there was in the exile so great a difference between the mass and the spiritual remnant as to account for the language of the passage. While they felt the national calamity to be traceable to the sin of the people, there is nothing to justify the view that they were the special object of the divine wrath.

---

[13] Der Messias, Gottingen, 1929, p.307.

The pious did not suffer *for*, but only *with*, the nation. Of the Servant it is said that *"he let his life blood flow unto death"*, but the spiritual Israel did not die in captivity.

Finally, the view that the Servant personifies the ideal Israel, existing at present only in the mind and purpose of God and becoming a reality only in the future, is also untenable. In the passage the actual nation is depicted realistically, with all its faults and its greatest sin – the rejection of the Servant, the Redeemer. Do lowly origin, mean appearance, and general repulsiveness characterize the ideal Israel? Can the ideal Israel suffer and die for the actual nation and rise again?

But in some other Servant passages[14] is not Israel called the Servant? While that is true, *the personality of the Servant in Isaiah 52:13 – 53:12 differs in kind from that of the Servant Israel* and towers in its grandeur above any other individual in the Old Testament. Then suffering has here new meaning – *necessity, purpose* and

---

[14] 41:8,9; 44:1,2; 45:4; 48:20; 49:3.

value. Israel's relationship to God was interrupted, when the nation became unfaithful.[15] The term "Servant of the Lord", originally identified with the nation Israel, in transcending its former national limitations, became associated with the person and office of the Messiah, who was entrusted with the mission in which Israel so ignominiously failed. Therefore, in a number of passages[16] the application of "Servant of the Lord" to the actual Israel is untenable, as in them the Servant is distinguished from Israel in having a mission to fulfil – to gather Israel and be a light to the world.

It is a striking fact that the synagogue readings from the prophets always omit the passage from Isaiah 52:12 through 53, while portions immediately preceding and following are read. If the leaders of modern Jewry really believe that this chapter depicts Israel, why do they not read it in public? At a memorial service for Jews perished in the gas chambers of Treblinka and Auschwitz-Buna, or in desperate fighting in the

---

[15] 42:18-20.
[16] 42:1-7; 49:1-9; 50:4-9.

Warsaw ghetto, what could be more comforting than the divine promise: *"My servant justifies many, / And bears their sin"?* To thousands who mourn relatives lost in the Nazi fury, how consoling would be the assurance that their loved one's deaths were part of a redemptive plan!

2. *The Individual Theory*

Some scholars holding the individual theory consider the Servant a leper or a martyr. No leper could have made the offering for sin so clearly described in the passage; even the animals sacrificed in the temple were without blemish. How can the words, *"By violence and death was he borne away"* (vs.8a), which imply a convict, and *"Though he worked no evil, / And spoke no guile"* (vs.9c,d), delineating miscarriage of justice, and *"That he was rapt from the land of the living"* (8c), suggesting in the original Hebrew, an idiom, *violent death,* be applied to a leper? Also where in history is there a record of such a leper? Some have seen in the passage the portrayal of a martyr, as Isaiah, or Jeremiah. But such a glorification of a pious man, even though he be a martyr, and particularly the idea that his death would result in the redemption of the Gentile world, is in itself foreign to the Old Testament, where one would search in vain for a eulogy of even the greatest of Israel's heroes, whether it be Abraham, Joseph, Moses or David.

Strong voices have been raised in support of the view that the Servant is the Messiah. As is evidenced from rabbinic literature including the prayers of the synagogue, the Old Synagogue was aware of the fact that the prophet is speaking of a person of transcendent influence, who morally and spiritually ranks above any other character in the Old Testament, and it applied the passage to the Messiah.

August Wunsche, in his book, *Die Leiden des Messias, h*as made a laborious compilation of extracts from old rabbinical writings from which the conclusion may be drawn that the conception of a suffering Messiah was by no means foreign to the Old Synagogue.[17]

---

[17] Cf. especially Sanhedrin 93a and 98b, quoted on pp. 56, 57, 62ff.

The renowned scholar Emil Schurer makes a similar reference:

> It is indisputable that in the second century after Christ, at least in certain circles of Jewry, there was familiarity with the idea of a Messiah who was to suffer, even suffer vicariously, for human sin. The portrayal of Justin makes it sure that Jewish scholars, through disputations with Christians, saw themselves forced to this concession. Thus an idea was applied to the Messiah which was familiar to rabbinic Judaism, that is, that the righteous man not only observes all the laws, but through suffering also atones for sins that may have been committed, and that the surplus suffering of the righteous benefits others.[18]

The *Targum Yonathan ben Uzziel* (first century), a paraphrase of the prophets, recognised in

---

[18] Geschichte des Judischen Valkes im Zeitalter Jesu Christi, 4th edit., Leipzig, 1907, vol. ii, p.650.

Babylonia as early as the third century and generally acknowledged as an ancient authority a century later, opens up the prophecy (Isaiah 52:13 – 53:12) thus: *"Behold my servant, the Messiah, prospers."* It shows striking inconsistencies , no doubt, because of later emendations, in applying some portions of the passage – the glory – to the Messiah, and other portions – the suffering – to Israel, but nevertheless it leaves no doubt that the Messiah gives His life for the redemption of Israel.

In *Midrash Cohen,* Elijah thus comforts the Messiah:

> Bear the suffering and the punishment of the Lord with which He chastises Thee for the sins of Israel, as it is written. "He is verily pierced for our rebellion, / Crushed for our iniquities" (Isaiah 53:5), until the end comes.[19]

---

[19] Driver-Neubauer, *The fifty-third chapter of Isaiah according to Jewish Interpreters,* Oxford, 1877, p.337.

The *Midrash Rabbah* of Rabbi Mosheh Haddarshan states:

Immediately the Holy One, blessed be He, began to put before the Messiah these stipulations, "Messiah, my righteous one, the sins of those hidden with thee will bring thee under a heavy yoke: Thine eyes will not see light; Thine ears will hear great reproach from the nations of the world; Thy nostrils will smell stench; Thy mouth will taste bitterness; Thy tongue will cleave to thy palate; Thy skin will shrivel upon Thy bone, and Thy soul will be weakened by grief and groaning. If thou are willing to take it upon thyself, well and good, but, if not, I shall drive them (the generations) out of existence even now." He answered, "Lord of the universe, I joyfully take upon myself these sufferings…" Immediately the Messiah took upon Himself "the sufferings of love", as it is said, "Torments willingly and humbly He endured." (Isaiah 53:7).[20]

---

[20] The passage is quoted only in Martin, Raymund, *Pugio Fidei,* Leipzig, 1687, p.416.

Another Midrash states that in the Messianic age the patriarchs will say to the Messiah:

> Ephraim, Messiah our Righteousness, although we are the forefathers, Thou art better than we, because Thou hast borne our iniquities and the iniquities of our children, and there have passed over Thee hardships such as have not passed upon men of earlier or of later time, and Thou wast an object of derision and contumely to the heathen for Israel's sake.[21]

The Musaph service for the Day of Atonement contains a remarkable ancient prayer:[22]

> Messiah our Righteousness has departed from us. Horror has seized us; for there is

_____

[21]*P'siqtha Rabbathi*, xxxvii, ed. Friedman, f. 161b-162a, quoted in full in Yalqut on Isaiah 60. 499.

[22] Levy, David, *Prayers for the Day of Atonement,* second edition, London, 1807, vol.III, p.38.

none to justify us. He bears our sins and the yoke of our iniquities, and is pierced for our transgressions. He bears our guilt on His shoulders, that He may win forgiveness for our sins. He is wounded for our salvation. O, Eternal One, it is time that Thou shouldest create Him anew! O, bring Him up from the terrestrial sphere. Raise Him up from the land of Seir,[23] to assemble us on Mount Lebanon[24], a second time, by the power of Yinnon![25]

The Celebrated Raymund Martin, in his work, *Pugio Fidei* (ca. 1278), has made many compilations from old rabbinical MSS., now

---

[23] Seir represents Edom, which in the Talmud is a synonym for Rome, where, according to Hebrew tradition, the Messiah undergoes humiliation and suffering.

[24] Lebanon symbolises the Mount of the Temple, where the Messiah is to appear.

[25] Yinnon is a Talmudic term for the Messiah in His pre-existent life, as in Psalm 72:17, which the Talmud renders, "Before the sun (was created), Yinnon was His name" (*Bab.Sanhedrin* 98b).

either no longer extant or transmitted to us in emended form, the accuracy of which such an authority as the late Professor E.B. Pusey of Oxford does not doubt, in which Isaiah 53 is applied to the Messiah.

In spite of the voices raised in the Old Synagogue, the illustrious scholar Rabbi Sh'lomoh Yizhaqi, better known from his initials as Rashi (ca. 1040-1105), followed by the great grammarian David Kimhi, (1160-1235), interpreted Isaiah 53 as referring to Israel. Rashi's position became authoritative in Jewry, but this is readily understood. If he wrote his commentary on Isaiah after 1095, when the Council of Clermont initiated the First Crusade, the massacres of Jews accompanying it very probably influenced him in taking Israel to be the Suffering Servant. The theory of Rashi and Kimhi was rejected as unsatisfactory by so great a scholar as Rabbi Mosheh ben Maimon, popularly known as Maimonides, or, from his initials, as Rambam (1135-1204), whose opinion finds justification in the Jewish liturgy, bearing the authority of the synagogue.

Not only in the Old Synagogue but as late as the seventeenth century leading rabbis, in harmony with the Jewish liturgy, applied the chapter to the Messiah. Rabbi Naphtali Ben Asher Altschuler (late sixteenth and early seventeenth centuries) states:

> I am surprised that Rashi and David Kimhi have not, with the Targum, also applied them (vss 52:13-53:12) to the Messiah.[26]

The following is from the pen of Rabbi Altschuler's contemporary, Rabbi Mosheh Alshekh, a disciple of the renowned Rabbi Joseph Caro, author of the *Shulhan 'Arukh:*

> I may remark, then, that our rabbis with one voice accept and affirm the opinion that the prophet is speaking of the King-Messiah, and we ourselves shall also adhere to the same view.[27]

---

[26] Driver-Neubauer, *opus cit.*, p.319.
[27] *Ibid.*, p.258

But who is the atoning Messiah of whom the prophet is speaking? History knows of no one but Jesus of Nazareth, who fulfilled all the predictions of Isaiah 53. Through Him God revealed himself and entered the course of human history. Only He was good enough and great enough to effect the atonement for the whole world. Only as we recognise in the awe-inspiring delineation His features do the blurring contradictions vanish away. That the Suffering Servant presents a perfect picture of Jesus the Messiah is sustained by the following:

1. He was a historic person (Matthew 2:1).

2. He was an innocent sufferer (John 8:46).

3. He was a voluntary sufferer (John 10:17,18; Galatians 2:20).

4. He was an obedient, humble, and silent sufferer (Matthew 27:12, 14; Philippians 2:8; 1 Peter 2:23).

5. His suffering was grounded in love. In Christ is manifested the redeeming and reconciling love of God (John 3:16), in which His atoning work was accomplished. Hence His words from the Cross: *"Father, forgive them; for they know no what they do"* (Luke 23:34).

6. His suffering was the result of a divine plan and fulfils the divine intentional will. God willed the redemption through Jesus Christ according to the eternal purpose of the *aeons* (Ephesians 3:11).

7. His suffering was vicarious (1 Peter 2:24).

8. His suffering was redemptive – a revelation of the arm of the Lord – that is, divine intervention in the course of history, leading to the justification of the evildoers from their sin (1 Corinthians 1:30, 1 Peter 1:18,19).

9. His suffering ended in death (Matthew 27:50).

10. His death gave way to resurrection (1 Corinthians 15:4).

11. The redemptive purpose of God, realised in the life, death, and resurrection of Christ, will be brought to full fruition at His Second Coming, when Israel's national confession and repentance will take place (Zechariah 12:10; Matthew 24:30,31; Romans 11:25,26).

12. He ascended into heaven and is now highly exalted, sitting at the right hand of God (John 1:51; Philippians 2:9-11).

Modern scholarship advocates the *composite view,* which regards the Servant simultaneously as Israel and as Jesus Christ. This is a mixture of error and truth. The New Testament clearly applies Isaiah fifty-three solely to Jesus Christ.[28]

---

[28] Matt.8:17; Mark 15:28; Luke 4:16ff; Luke 22:37; John 12:37,38; Acts 8:32,33,35; Hebrews 9:28; 1 Pet. 2:22-25.

We cannot here enter into a detailed examination of the objections to the fact that the Servant is Jesus Christ. Suffice it to say that they reveal a fundamental failure to take into consideration the twofold nature of Christ, the human and the divine, which are not mutually exclusive, and to comprehend the twofold purpose of His ministry – to suffer and to die, and then to rise triumphantly and take His exalted place at the right hand of God, as Isaiah predicted:

Behold, my servant prospers and is exalted;
He is lifted; he is raised high.

The Nature
of the
Challenge

The Nature of the Challenge

The leading idea in Isaiah 53 is the *atonement* effected by the Servant. Since this is the supreme event in the life of the Lord Jesus Christ, a brief discussion of the atonement is proper.

Proceeding from a free choice and breaking a divine command, sin attacks divine authority and breaks the existing unity between God and men, hence its serious consequences. It "pays a wage, and the wage is death" (Romans 6:23 N.E.B). To the Hebrews sacrifice was the expression of faith in God, faith in His *justice* in meting out the deserved death penalty for sin on the substitutionary victim, and faith in His *grace* of forgiveness. The idea of vicarious suffering was current among them, since it underlay their entire sacrificial system, which taught that a righteous God could make no compromise with sin, but must punish it by its merited recompense, death. But since God is also merciful, He has by grace instituted a means whereby sin may be atoned for through sacrifice, without violation of righteousness; for were He to pardon merely out of compassion, or because a sovereign being may do as he wills, He would undermine the moral structure of the universe.

Moreover, not only does the atonement appear to be the only righteous means of dealing with the problem of sin, but, because of its regenerating power, it is also the only efficacious way. Only after awful suffering and death does the Man of sorrows restore righteousness and bestow *new life*. The passage clearly implies that this redemption could not be effected by the Servant's teaching alone, since it is only *after he lays down his life for sin's atonement* that "*A long posterity he shall have; And he shall consummate the will of the Lord*".

The Old Testament ritual of sacrifice was a type of the sacrifice on Calvary. The blood of animals expiated sin only because it foreshadowed the vicarious sacrifice of Jesus Christ, whose death on the Cross provides the actual atonement typified by every sacrificial ritual and predicted by Isaiah, who declares in the fifty-third chapter that the Messiah is to make, or be, an 'asham, a guilt offering. In the vicarious atonement of Christ, God's compassion is manifested and the sinner is pardoned; and yet, in consistency with the rectitude of the divine government, sin is punished. Only the Lord Jesus Christ could make a valid atonement; for in Him we have not a mere man, who, because of His unique personality and matchless life, commands our following, or a martyr, who, in dying for His fellow-men, inspires our veneration. We have God incarnate coming down to man and Himself accomplishing the work of redemption.

The doctrine of the atonement is not a mere theological abstraction, apart from life. The God of all wisdom, who knows the human heart better than does man, also knows the best remedy. It has been seen that the anointing work of the Servant is followed by confession and repentance of the erring people. Throughout the ages men and women obedient to the divine will and willing to accept the salvation provided by God have found in the atonement "a power of God", which regenerated and transformed their lives. In committing themselves to God, they have become friends of God. *The new life in Christ is practical proof for the efficiency of the atonement,* which presents the mystery that not only does the innocent Servant suffer and die, but that His suffering and death are ordained by a righteous and loving God. Suffering and death lead to victory and glory (Isaiah 53:10-12). Therefore the atonement is a moral necessity in the divine plan for human redemption.

But does God forgive sin apart from blood atonement? Some rabbis teach that in cases where the Mosaic Law prescribes capital punishment, in the words of Scripture, *"that soul shall be cut off from Israel",*[29] the sole efficacy of repentance and of the Day of Atonement is that of suspension of the sentence, and the final expiation is achieved by suffering and death. They hold that the sin of profanation of the name of heaven (God) is atoned for to the extent of one-third by repentance and the Day of

---

[29] Exodus 12:15

Atonement, one third by bodily suffering during the remainder of the year, while nothing less than death can accomplish the final expiation.[30] The tradition of the School of Ishmael teaches that sins are atoned for by suffering: "Chastisements wipe out all a man's wickedness."[31] According to another tradition, the efficiency of suffering is greater than that of sacrifice, for the former is personal, while the latter concerns man's property.[32]

More than this, Judaism teaches that the suffering and death of the righteous effect atonement also for others. In *The Fourth Book of Maccabees* there is recorded a prayer ascribed to the martyr Eleazar:

> Thou knowest, O God, that when I might be saved, I am dying in fiery tortures on account of Thy law. Be gracious to Thy

---

[30] T *os. Yoma*, v.6-8; Babylo*nian Talmud*, "*Yoma*", 86a; Bacher*, Tannaiten*, I, 258; cf. Isa. 22:14.

[31] *Berakot*, v. a, end; cf *sifre Deut.* 32 (ed.Friedman, f.73b).

[32] Sifre.i.c.

people and satisfied with my punishment in their behalf. *Make my blood a sacrifice for their purification,* and take my life for a substitute for theirs.[33]

In conclusion the author thus affirms the idea of substitutionary suffering:

These, therefore, being sanctified for God's sake, were honoured with not only this honour,[34] but also in that for their sake the enemies did not have power over the nation, and the tyrant was punished, and the fatherland purified, they having become, as it were, *a substitute, dying for the sin of the nation;* and through the blood of those godly men and their propitiatory death divine Providence saved Israel, which was before in an ill plight.[35]

A clear distinction must be made between the Mosaic doctrine of the atonement and the

---

[33] 6:27-29.
[34] Heavenly rank near the throne of God.
[35] 17:20-22.

rabbinical teaching, often contradictory, which gradually took form in later centuries. The prayer of Eleazar is impressive, but out of harmony with the Scriptures. Neither penance, nor good works, nor physical death, even that of a martyr, can satisfy the perfect law of God, for *"there is none that doeth good, no, not one"* (Psalm 14:3; cf. Romans 3:12).

Every transgression deserves the divine wrath and curse, in this world and in the world to come. Physical death is part of the punishment for sin: it has no atoning efficacy for a third, or a half, or indeed any part of man's sin. After death, the predicted consequence of man's sin, comes the judgement. If all men have transgressed, as the Old Testament distinctly teaches, and if no man can make atonement for his own sin which is acceptable to a just God, it follows that works of supererogation are impossible, far less an atonement for others.

Although mediaeval rabbis wrote lengthy penitential prayers, which are still read before and on the Day of Atonement, among the masses the consciousness of sin and the need of salvation grow more and more faint. Then, as a result of Judaism's polemic with the Christian church, the idea of a suffering atoning Redeemer, by no means strange to the Old Synagogue, also became increasingly unwelcome.

Some scholars take issue with the atonement on moral grounds, *but the consciousness of guilt and the longing for expiation are universal in human experience.* Not only the Scriptures, but even the novelist and the dramatist emphasize this basic truth. It is also taught by all schools of psychology that among the three major causes of every anxiety neurosis, next to the sense of meaninglessness is the sense of guilt. The principle of an individual's bearing the guilt of the community has no connotation of injustice, since the divine judgement on sin is *willingly* accepted and endured by the blameless Servant of the Lord.

Although some may find the idea of one suffering for others abhorrent, there is no moral impropriety, when love steps in voluntarily to suffer and to save the sinner from the just consequence of transgression, as there is no moral impropriety, when the creditor remits a debt and thus himself becomes the loser. More than this, the basic law of redemption through sacrifice operates in the entire world. The mineral sacrifices itself for the vegetable, the vegetable for the animal, and the animal for man. This however, must not be construed as similar in kind to the sacrifice of the Lord Jesus Christ, which does not have its counterpart in nature and is unique.

If atonement be a moral necessity for mankind as a whole, it must also be so for every member of the human race. To appropriate it and make it one's own, each person must make a commitment and in trust and submission embrace the redemption provided by God in the atonement of Christ at Calvary. Divine love has flung down a challenge, in the face of which neutrality is impossible, and more – dangerous, as divine justice will hold each human soul accountable for an answer.

Come to the Saviour now,
  He gently calleth thee;
In true repentance bow,
  Before Him bend the knee;
He waiteth to bestow,
  Salvation, peace and love,
True joy on earth below,
  A home in heaven above.

Come to the Saviour now,
  Ye who have wandered far;
Renew your solemn vow,
  For His by right you are;
Come, like poor wandering sheep
  Returning to his fold;
His arm will safely keep,
  His love will ne'er grow cold.

More about Jesus Christ

More about Jesus Christ

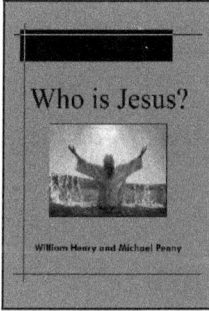

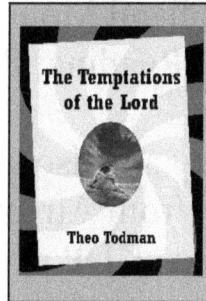

Jesus: God and Man
Brian Sherring

Who is Jesus?
W M Henry and Michael Penny

The Temptations of the Lord
Theo Todman

The Virgin Birth
Theo Todman

Please note:

Further details of all the books mentioned can be
seen on **www.obt.org.uk**

The can be ordered from the website
and also from

The Open Bible Trust,
Fordland Mount, Upper Basildon,
Reading, RG8 8LU, UK.

They are also available as eBooks
from Amazon and Apple,
and also as KDP paperbacks from Amazon.

Search Magazine

Michael Penny is editor of *Search* magazine

About this Book

Isaiah 53
Who is the
Suffering Servant?

The earliest Christian understanding of Isaiah 53 was that the *Suffering Servant* was Jesus Christ. However, that view has been challenged, especially by some modern Jewish teachers.

With scholarship and reverence, the author has contested the validity of their challenge, showing their views not to be in harmony with Scripture. He has also, at the same time, given us a good defence of the fact that Jesus Christ was, indeed, the *Suffering Servant.*

9 781783 644896